FRIENDS
OF ACPL

3/04

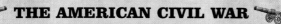

THE AMERICAN CIVIL WAR

Major Battles of the Civil War

A MyReportlinks.com Book

Kim A. O'Connell

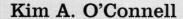

MyReportLinks.com Books

an imprint of

Enslow Publishers, Inc. **E**

Box 398, 40 Industrial Road
Berkeley Heights, NJ 07922
USA

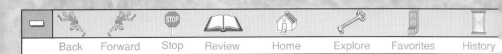
MyReportLinks.com Books, an imprint of Enslow Publishers, Inc. MyReportLinks®
is a registered trademark of Enslow Publishers, Inc.

Library of Congress Cataloging-in-Publication Data

O'Connell, Kim A.
  Major battles of the Civil War / Kim A. O'Connell.
     p. cm. — (The American Civil War)
Summary: Reviews the critical battles of the Civil War, providing
background information on the causes and a glimpse of the changes
brought about by this war between the states. Includes Internet links to
Web sites related to the Civil War.
Includes bibliographical references and index.
  ISBN 0-7660-5187-0
  1. United States—History—Civil War, 1861–1865—Campaigns—Juvenile
literature. [1. United States—History—Civil War,
1861-1865—Campaigns.] I. Title. II. American Civil War (Berkeley
Heights, N.J.)
  E470.O28 2004
  973.7'3—dc22
                              2003013306

Printed in the United States of America

10 9 8 7 6 5 4 3 2 1

To Our Readers:
Through the purchase of this book, you and your library gain access to the Report Links that specifically back
up this book.
The Publisher will provide access to the Report Links that back up this book and will keep these Report Links
up to date on **www.myreportlinks.com** for three years from the book's first publication date.
We have done our best to make sure all Internet addresses in this book were active and appropriate when we
went to press. However, the author and the Publisher have no control over, and assume no liability for, the
material available on those Internet sites or on other Web sites they may link to.
The usage of the MyReportLinks.com Books Web site is subject to the terms and conditions stated on the
Usage Policy Statement on **www.myreportlinks.com**.
A password may be required to access the Report Links that back up this book. The password is found on the
bottom of page 4 of this book.
Any comments or suggestions can be sent by e-mail to comments@myreportlinks.com or to the address on
the back cover.

Photo Credits: © Hemera Technologies, Inc., 1997–2001, p. 9 (flags); Defense Visual Information
Center/National Archives and Records Administration, pp. 21, 36, 42, 44; Enslow Publishers, Inc.,
pp. 12, 17, 32; Library of Congress, pp. 1, 3, 24, 26, 28, 29, 38, 40; MyReportLinks.com Books, p.
4, back cover; National Park Service, p. 11; The American Civil War.com, pp. 31, 35; The Gilder
Lehrman Institute of American History/The Chicago Historical Society, pp. 15, 19, 23.

Cover Photo: Flags, © Hemera Technologies, Inc., 1997–2001; all other images, Library of Congress.

Cover Description: Battle painting: Battle of Antietam, Library of Congress.

Contents

About MyReportLinks.com Books

MyReportLinks.com Books
Great Books, Great Links, Great for Research!

The Report Links listed on the following four pages can save you hours of research time by **instantly** bringing you to the best Web sites relating to your report topic.

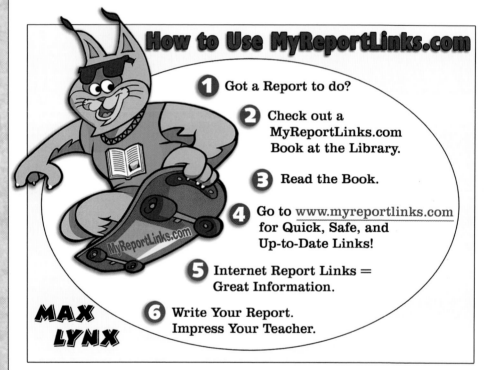

How to Use MyReportLinks.com

1 Got a Report to do?

2 Check out a MyReportLinks.com Book at the Library.

3 Read the Book.

4 Go to www.myreportlinks.com for Quick, Safe, and Up-to-Date Links!

5 Internet Report Links = Great Information.

6 Write Your Report. Impress Your Teacher.

MAX LYNX

The pre-evaluated Web sites are your links to source documents, photographs, illustrations, and maps. They also provide links to dozens—even hundreds—of Web sites about your report subject.

MyReportLinks.com Books and the MyReportLinks.com Web site save you time and make report writing easier than ever!

Please see "To Our Readers" on the copyright page for important information about this book, the MyReportLinks.com Web site, and the Report Links that back up this book. Please enter **WMB8172** if asked for a password.

Report Links

The Internet sites described below can be accessed at
http://www.myreportlinks.com

▶**Antietam on the Web**   *EDITOR'S CHOICE*

This site provides information about the bloodiest single day of fighting
in American history—the Battle of Antietam, in Maryland, which took
place on September 17, 1862.

▶**CWSAC Battle Summaries**   *EDITOR'S CHOICE*

This Web site provides summaries of all the battles fought in the Civil
War. Each summary includes a description of the battle, including the
dates, key figures, and other statistics.

▶**The American Civil War**   *EDITOR'S CHOICE*

This site provides information about the major battles of the Civil War,
along with additional information about the battlefields. You will also
find biographies, maps, and photos.

▶**Civil War Map Collection**   *EDITOR'S CHOICE*

The Library of Congress Web site holds a collection of Civil War maps,
many showing the areas in which battles were fought.

▶**Appomattox Court House**   *EDITOR'S CHOICE*

At this National Park Service Web site you will learn about the house at
Appomattox Court House where Robert E. Lee surrendered to Ulysses
S. Grant, bringing an end to the major battles of the Civil War.

▶**The Civil War**   *EDITOR'S CHOICE*

This site, based on the award-winning PBS series, provides a
comprehensive look at the Civil War. Here you will find images, battle
descriptions, historical documents, and facts about the war.

Report Links

The Internet sites described below can be accessed at http://www.myreportlinks.com

▶American Originals

The National Archives and Records Administration Web site provides information about the 54th Massachusetts Infantry, an African-American regiment that fought valiantly at Fort Wagner, South Carolina.

▶Antietam National Battlefield

At this National Park Service Web site you will learn about the Battle of Antietam, the bloodiest single day of fighting in United States history, and view pictures of the battlefield as it now stands.

▶The Battle of Fredericksburg

This PBS site offers a brief overview of the Battle of Fredericksburg, which took place in November 1863. In particular, it gives five reasons why Union general Ambrose Burnside's battle plan failed.

▶The Battle of Gettysburg

This site contains a description of the pivotal battle of the Civil War: the Battle of Gettysburg, fought over three days in July 1863, in southwestern Pennsylvania. You will also find the official records from the battle from both the Union and Confederate sides.

▶Civil War @ Smithsonian

This Web site from the Smithsonian Institution contains images and descriptions of Civil War portraits, weapons, and other objects.

▶Civil War Treasures

Civil War Treasures, a Library of Congress Web site, explores the Civil War through images, manuscripts, posters, and writings.

▶Crisis at Fort Sumter

This site provides a detailed account of the steps leading to the outbreak of war between the North and South.

▶Fifty-fourth Massachusetts Infantry

This site provides a brief history of the 54th Massachusetts Infantry, a famous regiment of African-American troops that fought in the Civil War.

Any comments? Contact us: **comments@myreportlinks.com**

Report Links

The Internet sites described below can be accessed at http://www.myreportlinks.com

▶**General Robert E. Lee**

This site features a biography of General Robert E. Lee, the South's leading general in the Civil War and considered by many one of the greatest military figures in American history. Included are links to photos and other articles about Lee.

▶**George McClellan**

This site provides a biography of General George McClellan. Links within the text will direct you to additional information about him.

▶**The Gettysburg Address**

At this Library of Congress Web site you will find drafts of the Gettysburg Address, which was delivered by Abraham Lincoln on November 19, 1863, during the dedication of the national cemetery at Gettysburg.

▶**A House Divided: America in the Age of Lincoln**

This online exhibit focuses on American life in the years of Abraham Lincoln's presidency (1861 to 1865).

▶**John Brown's Holy War**

This PBS Web site contains the story of John Brown and the Harpers Ferry raid. Here you will find interactive maps, biographies, a time line, and other resources.

▶**Lincoln's Challenge, 1864**

This Web site describes some of the conflicts, including civil war, that Abraham Lincoln faced in the election of 1864.

▶**Lincoln's Secret Weapon**

This PBS site explores the Union's ironclad battleship the USS *Monitor*. Learn about its history and take a virtual tour of the ship.

▶**Manassas**

At this National Park Service Web site you can explore the history of Manassas National Battlefield Park and learn about the two battles that took place there.

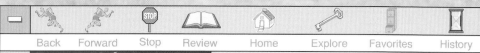
Report Links

The Internet sites described below can be accessed at http://www.myreportlinks.com

▶**"Never Was I So Depressed"—James Longstreet and Pickett's Char**

This Gettysburg National Military Park site includes a comprehensive article on Confederate general James Longstreet and the attack at Gettysburg that has become known as Pickett's Charge.

▶**Petersburg National Battlefield: The Battle of the Crater**

This site offers an account of the Battle of the Crater, during the siege of Petersburg, Virginia. The Union strategy of exploding a mine and building a tunnel to rip through the Confederate defenses resulted in thousands of Union casualties.

▶**Selected Civil War Photographs**

From this Library of Congress Web site you will find images of the Civil War as well as a time line of the war.

▶**Sherman's March to the Sea**

This site contains letters and images of Union general William Tecumseh Sherman from his Georgia campaign as well as articles about his famous "march to the sea."

▶**Stonewall Jackson Resources: VMI Archives**

The Stonewall Jackson Resources Web site is a comprehensive resource for information on the famous Confederate general. Here you will learn about his life and role in the Civil War.

▶**Today in History: Lee Surrenders**

This Library of Congress site describes the events of April 9, 1865, in which General Robert E. Lee surrendered the Army of Northern Virginia to Ulysses S. Grant.

▶**Ulysses S. Grant in Battle**

At the Ulysses S. Grant in Battle Web site you will find links to information about the battles he fought in during the Civil War.

▶**Vicksburg National Military Park**

At this National Park Service Web site you will learn about the battle for Vicksburg and find images and maps of the historic park.

Major Battle Facts

Battle Name and Date*	Union Casualties	Confederate Casualties	Location	Victor
First Manassas (Bull Run) July 21, 1861	2,896	1,982	Manassas, Va.	CSA
USS *Monitor* /CSS *Virginia* March 8–9, 1862	409	24	Hampton Roads, Va.	Draw
Shiloh April 6–7, 1862	13,047	10,699	Hardin County, Tenn.	USA
Gaines Mill (largest Seven Days battle) June 27, 1862	6,837	8,750	Richmond, Va.	CSA
Second Manassas (Bull Run) August 28–30, 1862	13,826	8,353	Manassas, Va.	CSA
Antietam September 17, 1862	12,400	10,300	Sharpsburg, Md.	USA
Fredericksburg December 11–15, 1862	12,600	5,300	Fredericksburg, Va.	CSA
Chancellorsville April 30–May 6, 1863	18,000	12,800	Chancellorsville, Va.	CSA
Vicksburg May 18–July 4, 1863	4,835	32,697	Vicksburg, Miss.	USA
Gettysburg July 1–3, 1863	23,000	28,000	Gettysburg, Pa.	USA
Fort Wagner July 18, 1863	1,515	222	Morris Island, S.C.	CSA
Chickamauga Sept. 18–20, 1863	16,170	18,454	Chickamauga, Ga.	CSA
Chattanooga Nov. 23–25, 1863	5,815	6,667	Chattanooga, Tenn.	USA
Wilderness May 5–6, 1864	18,000	10,800	Near Fredericksburg, Va.	Draw
Spotsylvania Court House May 8–21, 1864	18,000	9–10,000	Spotsylvania County, Va.	Draw
Cold Harbor June 1–12, 1864	13,000	3,000	Hanover County, Va.	CSA
Atlanta Aug. 31–Sept. 1, 1864	1,149	2,000	Atlanta, Ga.	USA
Petersburg April 2, 1865	3,894	4,852	Petersburg, Va.	USA
Sailor's Creek April 6, 1865	1,148	7,700	Farmville, Va.	USA

* The statistics for this page were compiled from *The Civil War Battlefield Guide* by Francis H. Kennedy, second edition, New York, Houghton Mifflin Co., 1998.

Chapter 1

The Bloodiest Day

On a late summer day in September 1862, the morning dawned foggy and warm near the small town of Sharpsburg, Maryland. The cornstalks in the fields were tall and plentiful, and the local farmers and shopkeepers were getting ready for their day. They could not know that their fields and lanes would soon be witness to the bloodiest single day of the Civil War.

In just over a year of fighting, the Confederate army leaders were feeling confident. They had won many key victories in Virginia, on their own soil. Confederate general Robert E. Lee wanted to take the war to the north to threaten the nation's capital at Washington, D.C., and draw the Union army out of Virginia. A northern campaign would also give Virginia's farmers the time they needed to gather their harvests, which would provide Lee's men with needed food for the coming winter. Finally, it was hoped that Confederate victories in the northern campaign would lead to Great Britain and France supporting the South.

The Southerners crossed the Potomac River in early September. They were so sure of victory that the soldiers splashed through the shallow river, shouting the famous "rebel yell." They met the Union forces, led by General George McClellan, on a field near Antietam Creek, a quiet stream that flowed past Sharpsburg. As the sun burned the fog away on September 17, fighting erupted through a thick cornfield, not far from the small, white

Historic Sketches of Antietam Battlefield - Microsoft Internet Explorer

File　Edit　View　Favorites　Tools　Help

Address ⓔ http://www.nps.gov/anti/sketches/sketch8.htm　　　　▾　⤳ Go　Links

Sketch by artist Frank Schell depicting Union soldiers fording Antietam Creek. First appeared in Frank Leslie's Illustrated Newspaper October 11, 1862. The soldiers are claimed to be part of General Hooker's First Corp on their way to "attack the Rebel army under General Lee."

Done　　　　　　　　　🌐 Internet

▲ *This color sketch of the Battle of Antietam shows Union soldiers under General Joseph Hooker crossing Antietam Creek on their way to attack General Robert E. Lee's Confederate forces.*

Dunker Church. The battle destroyed the cornfield as if it had been cut by hand. "Every stalk of corn in the greater part of the field was cut as closely as could have been done with a knife," Union general Joseph Hooker remembered later.[1] Soldiers had been cut down as well.

All day, the armies battered each other. With the sun high overhead, fighting centered on a sunken road that would later be renamed Bloody Lane. Here, hundreds on both sides lost their lives. Late in the afternoon, the armies faced each other across a stone bridge over Antietam Creek. Confederate sharpshooters set their sights on the

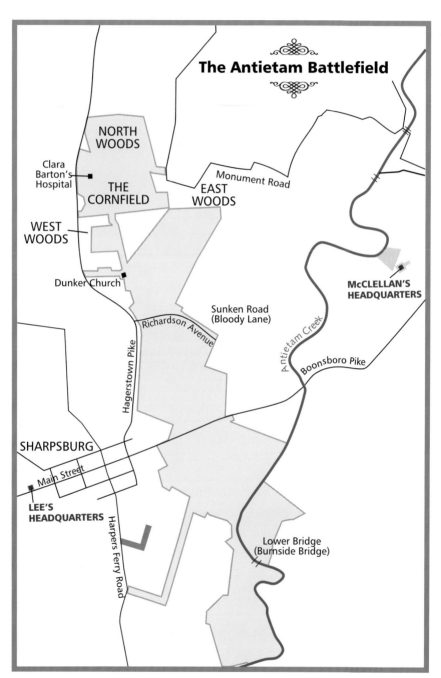

The Antietam Battlefield

NORTH WOODS

Clara Barton's Hospital

THE CORNFIELD

EAST WOODS

Monument Road

WEST WOODS

Dunker Church

McCLELLAN'S HEADQUARTERS

Sunken Road (Bloody Lane)

Richardson Avenue

Antietam Creek

Hagerstown Pike

Boonsboro Pike

SHARPSBURG

Main Street

LEE'S HEADQUARTERS

Harpers Ferry Road

Lower Bridge (Burnside Bridge)

▲ This map depicts the scene of battle on September 17, 1862, at Antietam.

approaches to the bridge, where they could easily target the Yankees trying to cross it. After several attempts, Union troops were able to cross the bridge and push back the Confederate army.

Suffering terrible losses, Lee had no choice but to retreat south to Virginia. The battle was considered a strategic victory for the Union. But victory came at great cost. In the end, one day of fighting had lost nearly twenty-three thousand men on both sides—seventeen thousand wounded and six thousand dead.

But the Battle of Antietam set in motion an important chain of events. President Abraham Lincoln had been looking for political support for the Emancipation Proclamation, which would go into effect on January 1, 1863. The victory at Antietam gave him that support—and he quickly issued a draft of the famous document promising freedom to slaves in the states that were under rebellion. Antietam also convinced Great Britain and France not to recognize the Confederacy as a separate nation and thus not send aid to its struggling army.

Together, these two events dealt a major blow to the Confederate cause. Although the Civil War would rage on for nearly three more years, the seeds of ultimate Union victory may have been planted in the fields of Antietam.

Chapter 2

The First Shots

At the beginning of the nineteenth century, Americans were united against a common enemy. They had won their independence from Great Britain in the Revolutionary War, and they were determined to keep it. By mid-century, however, sectional differences had developed between North and South. With its growing cities, the North, though still largely rural, depended on trade more than agriculture. The less populated South was dependent on cotton and tobacco farming and on slave labor. Southerners later argued that they fought the Civil War to defend states' rights—in which the states had more power than the federal government. But one "right" the South always defended was the practice of slavery.

▶ Calling for Abolition

The first Africans brought to America were considered indentured servants—they were promised freedom after working for a certain period of time. Over the seventeenth century, the colonies established laws making African Americans and their offspring slaves for life, although most Northern states had outlawed the practice by the eighteenth century's end. In the South, however, whenever questions arose about whether slavery should continue, new laws were enacted to keep the "peculiar institution" firmly in place.

By 1820, the United States had begun its westward expansion, and the leaders in government wondered whether slavery should continue in the new territories. That year the Missouri Compromise allowed the addition of Missouri, a slave state, to the Union, as the nation was often called then. To maintain a balance between the states that allowed slavery and those that did not, Maine was admitted as a free state. Slavery was prohibited in the vast territory obtained in the Louisiana Purchase that lay above 36 degrees 30 minutes north latitude, which marked the southern boundary of Missouri.

Increasingly, people known as abolitionists demanded the end of slavery. But the government tried to please both North and South. At mid-century, a series of bills that

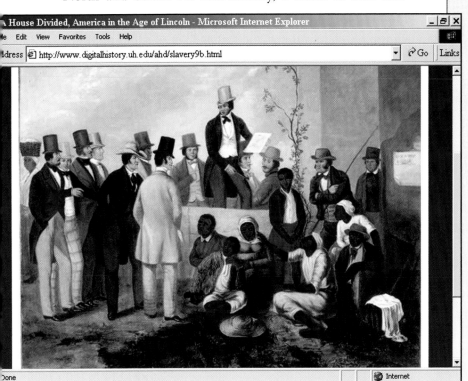

A House Divided, America in the Age of Lincoln - Microsoft Internet Explorer

File   Edit   View   Favorites   Tools   Help

Address http://www.digitalhistory.uh.edu/ahd/slavery9b.html   Go   Links

Done   Internet

▲ *The scene at an American slave auction was painted in 1852. Its sympathetic portrayal of the plight of African slaves came at a time when abolitionist sentiment was on the rise, following the publication of Harriet Beecher Stowe's* Uncle Tom's Cabin.

came to be known as the Compromise of 1850 organized much of the land gained through the Mexican-American War as territories without mention of slavery. The settlers of those territories would be left to decide about slavery once the territories became states. California was admitted to the Union as a free state, and the slave trade was banned from the nation's capital, but slavery could continue where it existed.

The most controversial part of the Compromise, which was added to appease Southerners for California's admittance as a free state, was the Fugitive Slave Act of 1850. It required citizens to return slaves who had escaped to their owners, and it denied fugitives the right to a trial by jury. That law angered many, especially abolitionists and others who had long been engaged in helping escaped slaves to seek freedom in the North and Canada through the Underground Railroad. This was not an actual railroad but a system or network of safe houses that led slaves to free lands.

Abolitionists became even more determined to oppose slavery in impassioned speeches and also in books. In 1852, Harriet Beecher Stowe published *Uncle Tom's Cabin*, a novel about the hardships of a good-hearted slave, which was an attack on the Fugitive Slave Act. Within a year, more than 300,000 copies were sold. Frederick Douglass, a former slave, gave frequent speeches against slavery. He spoke with such eloquence that his audience often found it hard to believe that he had once been a slave, since most slaves were deprived of education.

▶ Setbacks in Congress and Court

For every effort to abolish slavery, it seemed that an equally strong effort was made to keep it. In 1854, the

Kansas-Nebraska Act, which added the territories of Kansas and Nebraska from lands that had been promised to American Indians, allowed white citizens of those territories to decide whether to permit slavery there. Fighting in Kansas between antislavery and proslavery forces led to more than two hundred deaths.

The rights of African-American slaves were further diminished by a Supreme Court ruling in 1857. In the Dred Scott case, the U.S. Supreme Court ruled that Dred Scott as a slave had no rights as a citizen under the Constitution to seek freedom. Dred Scott was a Missouri

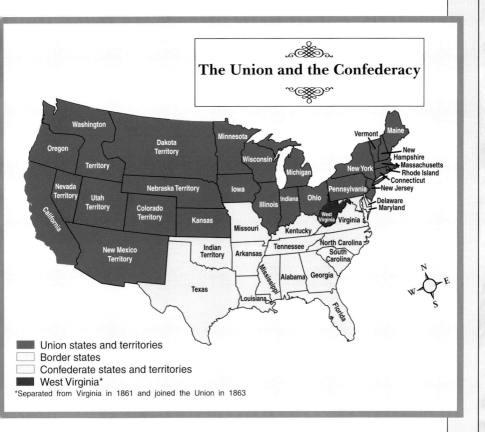

The Union and the Confederacy

- Union states and territories
- Border states
- Confederate states and territories
- West Virginia*

*Separated from Virginia in 1861 and joined the Union in 1863

This map of the United States shows the alignment of states—Union, Confederate, and border—during the Civil War.

slave who had sued his owner in 1846 for freedom on the grounds that he had been taken into Illinois, a free state, and into the Wisconsin Territory, which banned slavery. The Court ruled that Scott was not a citizen and that neither Congress nor any territorial government could ban slavery in any territory, which overturned the Missouri Compromise. This decision widened the gulf between North and South.

John Brown's Raid

Most abolitionists wanted a peaceful end to slavery. But an abolitionist named John Brown felt that violence was the only way to force an end to the practice. "Talk! Talk! Talk!" he said after one abolitionist meeting. "That will never free the slaves. What is needed is action—action."[1]

In 1859, Brown took action. With a band of men, he launched an attack on a Union weapons storehouse in Harpers Ferry, Virginia (now West Virginia), with the aim of arming slaves and gaining support for a revolt. When the attack failed, Brown was captured by a group of U.S. Marines, commanded by Robert E. Lee. Brown was executed for his crime, becoming a martyr to some, although his actions were condemned by many. Still, Southerners saw him as a symbol of sacrifice for the Northern cause. Later, a song called "John Brown's Body" would become a favorite marching tune for Union soldiers.

Secession

The following year, 1860, Abraham Lincoln, a lanky and awkward lawyer from Illinois, was elected president. Lincoln had promised to keep slavery from spreading into new states and territories where it did not already exist. Not surprisingly, Lincoln was not popular in the slave-holding South, and those states threatened to secede from, or leave, the Union if Lincoln was elected.

In December, South Carolina boldly made the first move and seceded from the Union. In February 1861, a convention of seceded states, including South Carolina, Mississippi, Florida, Alabama, Georgia, Louisiana, and Texas adopted the first constitution of the Confederate States of America. They elected a former senator from Mississippi named Jefferson Davis as the president of the Confederacy. Arkansas, Tennessee, Virginia, and North Carolina soon followed these states into the Confederacy. Although the first Confederate capital was in Montgomery, Alabama, it was moved to Richmond, Virginia, in May 1861.

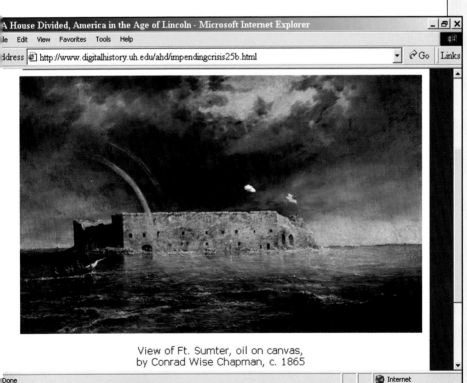

A House Divided, America in the Age of Lincoln - Microsoft Internet Explorer

File   Edit   View   Favorites   Tools   Help

Address http://www.digitalhistory.uh.edu/ahd/impendingcrisis25b.html   Go   Links

View of Ft. Sumter, oil on canvas,
by Conrad Wise Chapman, c. 1865

Done   Internet

A Confederate soldier painted this scene of Fort Sumter, at the time in Confederate hands.

Seven states had already left the Union by March 4, when Abraham Lincoln was inaugurated. At his inauguration, Lincoln made one last request that the South keep the peace. "In your hands, my dissatisfied countrymen, and not in mine is the momentous issue of civil war," he said. "The government will not assail you. You can have no conflict, without being yourselves the aggressors."[2] Lincoln also reaffirmed what he had earlier said in his campaign, that he would not threaten slavery where it already existed. Southern politicians doubted that promise, however, since Lincoln had also condemned slavery as evil.

Fort Sumter

Just over a month later, South Carolina became the aggressor, demanding the transfer to the state of all federal property within it, including Fort Sumter in Charleston Harbor. In the predawn darkness of April 12, 1861, Confederate troops fired the first shots of the war, attacking Union forces stationed in the fort. At first, the fort's commander refused to give up. But after exchanging cannon fire for a day, the Union troops finally surrendered on April 13, and the fort was evacuated by Union troops the day after.

Lincoln issued a call for troops, and Jefferson Davis did the same. Veteran soldiers of the U.S. Army, many of whom had served together fifteen years earlier in the Mexican-American War, were forced to choose sides. Thousands of new volunteers, eager to fight for their homelands and their beliefs, signed up as well. The Union boys, known as Yankees, were outfitted in crisp blue uniforms, while the Confederates, also known as rebels, dressed in varied, homespun uniforms of brown and gray.

The Civil War had begun.

Chapter 3

The Rise of the South: Battles From 1861 to 1862

In the early days of the war, some people did not take the fighting seriously. Spectators brought picnic baskets and sat on nearby hillsides to watch the war's first major battle, which took place near the town of Manassas, Virginia, along a stream called Bull Run. Even the soldiers who had enlisted did not expect the war to take very long. "I will not enlist for a longer period than three months," wrote a lieutenant from Pennsylvania, "unless my country needs me, in which event I would enlist for life."[1]

That soldier and many others found themselves fighting much longer than they had expected.

Confederate general Thomas Jonathan "Stonewall" Jackson is considered one of the great military strategists of the Civil War for his victories in the Valley campaign, at Fredericksburg, and at Second Manassas. His death came not at the hands of Union soldiers but his own men, when they mistook him for one of the enemy.

First Manassas or Bull Run

During the Civil War, the U.S. Army often named battles after landmarks or waterways, while the Confederacy named them after the closest town. As a result, many battles have more than one name. The war's first major land battle is known as both Manassas and Bull Run.

In June 1861, Union troops had slowly advanced from Washington, D.C., into northeastern Virginia, where Confederate soldiers waited for them at Manassas. When they clashed on July 21, soldiers in both armies were often confused about where to go and what to do. Thousands of men were killed and wounded. In the end, the Confederates held their ground, forcing the Union soldiers to retreat.

Confederate general Thomas J. Jackson was among the victors. A soldier, professor, and Virginia native, Jackson earned his famous nickname "Stonewall" in this battle. That name is supposed to have come when another general, Barnard Bee, urging his men to be strong, said, "There is Jackson standing like a stone wall! Rally behind the Virginians!"[2] Bee did not live to hear the nickname used, however—he was killed in the First Battle of Manassas.

The Battle of the Ironclads

In March 1862, a new age of naval warfare began with the battle at Hampton Roads, Virginia, of the ironclad ships the USS *Monitor* and the *Merrimac*. (The Confederate navy renamed the USS *Merrimac* the CSS *Virginia* after capturing the naval yard at Norfolk and raising the ship.)

The *Monitor*'s design was new, but the *Merrimac* was a wooden ship covered with iron plating that resisted enemy fire. The two ships shelled each other for four hours. Although the *Monitor* cracked the *Merrimac*'s iron plating in several spots, neither ship could punch a hole through the other. The battle ended with no clear victor. But this famous duel meant that all existing warships without iron sides were immediately outdated. Before the war was over, the Confederacy built twenty-one ironclads, and the Union constructed fifty-eight.

Shiloh

Although Virginia hosted a large share of the war's major battles, the Civil War was also fought in the states farther

A House Divided, America in the Age of Lincoln - Microsoft Internet Explorer

File   Edit   View   Favorites   Tools   Help

Address   http://www.digitalhistory.uh.edu/ahd/civilwar27b.html   Go   Links

Done   Internet

▲ *Ulysses S. Grant earned the nickname "Unconditional Surrender" Grant following his victories at Fort Donelson and Fort Henry. Those battles also earned him the respect of his commander-in-chief, Abraham Lincoln, although it would take Lincoln two more years to put Grant in command of all Union armies.*

west, in the areas between the Appalachian Mountains and the Mississippi River. Throughout the war, both armies competed for control of the Mississippi and other major waterways. If an army controlled key places along important rivers, it was harder for the enemy to move troops and supplies.

Early in 1862, Union general Ulysses S. Grant had won easy victories at Fort Henry on the Tennessee River and Fort Donelson on the Cumberland River. By early April, Grant's troops had moved down the Tennessee toward a town named Pittsburg Landing. There, soldiers pitched their tents near the small Shiloh Church and rested for the night. They were awakened early on April 6 by charging rebels and gunfire. Confederate general Albert Sidney Johnston had launched a surprise attack.

On the battle's first day, thousands of Union soldiers were killed. Later, some Yankees had reformed a battle line

▲ *The carnage from the Battle of Shiloh, with more than 23,000 killed or wounded in just two days, convinced both sides that the war would not come to a quick end.*

along a sunken road they called "the Hornet's Nest." By day's end, however, the survivors were forced to surrender.

But this had given Grant enough time to strengthen his army's position elsewhere. At dawn on April 7, Grant's army counterattacked, after receiving reinforcements from the Army of the Ohio under the command of General Don Carlos Buell. General Johnston was killed in the fighting, and the Confederate army began an exhausted retreat. Although Grant had won again, more than thirteen thousand Union soldiers and more than ten thousand Confederate soldiers were killed or wounded in just two days at the Battle of Shiloh.

This battle had turned the untrained recruits of the previous summer into hardened veterans. "Those who had stood shoulder to shoulder during the two terrible days of that bloody battle," a Shiloh veteran later wrote, "were hooped with steel, with bands stronger than steel."[3]

Shenandoah and Seven Days

By summer 1862, Stonewall Jackson had been marching his army doggedly through Virginia's Shenandoah Valley. There, Jackson's soldiers won a string of victories, protecting vital farm country for the Confederacy.

To the east, the Seven Days' Battles were raging near Richmond, the Confederate capital and a great prize for the Union if captured. Rebel troops under the command of Joseph E. Johnston defended the capital, but the fighting was bloody and led to no clear winner. After Johnston was wounded, command of the Army of Northern Virginia was given to Robert E. Lee, a loyal Virginian who was related by marriage to George Washington. At first, Union general George McClellan thought that the fifty-five-year-old Lee would be slow and cautious. He could not have been more

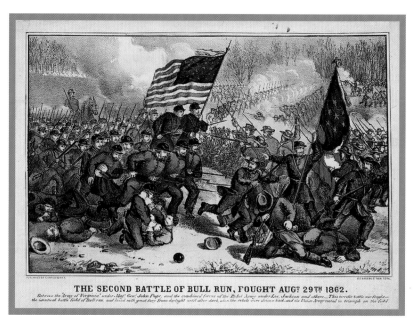

THE SECOND BATTLE OF BULL RUN, FOUGHT AUG. 29TH 1862.

▲ *This lithograph depicts the Second Battle of Manassas or Bull Run, a Confederate victory for Generals Robert E. Lee and Stonewall Jackson.*

wrong. Lee forced McClellan to retreat and kept the Confederate capital from falling into Union hands.

▶ Second Manassas or Bull Run

Late in the afternoon of August 28, 1862, the Second Battle of Manassas began, felling more than a third of all soldiers on that first day. The fighting grew even more deadly. At one point, Union forces led by Major General John Pope advanced toward Stonewall Jackson's men, who were protected by an unfinished railroad cut. The Union troops were defeated easily. "What a slaughter of men that was!" a soldier from Georgia recalled. "They were so thick it was just impossible to miss them."[4]

With this victory, the South regained control of nearly all of Virginia. The Confederacy began to believe that its independence would soon be won and that this new nation would be recognized by Europe and all the world.

Antietam

It was this confidence that led Lee and his army to the banks of Antietam Creek in Maryland. Yet that one day of bloodshed dealt a serious blow to the Confederacy—and gave the Union, and President Lincoln, a strategic victory. Not every Yankee could celebrate. Because General George McClellan failed to follow Lee as he retreated to Virginia, President Lincoln relieved him of his command. The Union army was now led by General Ambrose Burnside.

Fredericksburg

Burnside's first major test came in December 1862 as both armies faced each other in the town of Fredericksburg, Virginia, with only the wide Rappahannock River between them. Christmas was going to be difficult that year for many Fredericksburg residents, who were asked to leave for their own safety. The soldiers made the best of it, beginning a brisk trade across the river. Yankees sent sugar and coffee across in makeshift boats, and the rebels sent them back filled with tobacco.

When the attack order came, Union troops focused their charge on a hilly area of Fredericksburg called Marye's Heights. This was an ill-fated decision, because the rebels were safely protected by a stone wall, ready with their cannons. Wave after wave of Yankee soldiers were killed before Burnside finally halted the attack. The Union army suffered a terrible defeat, with more than twelve thousand casualties. Despite the Confederate victory, Lee was moved to remark to fellow Confederate general James Longstreet, "It is well the war is so terrible: we would grow too fond of it!"[5]

▲ *Robert E. Lee and his men are pictured surveying the scene at Fredericksburg. Although the battle ended in a Confederate victory, it proved a costly one in terms of men and supplies.*

Amid the bloodshed, however, there were acts of unexpected kindness. When the guns paused, a caring Confederate named Richard Kirkland risked being shot to bring water to wounded Union soldiers. He became known as the "Angel of Marye's Heights."

The North Pushes Back: Battles From 1863 to 1864

Both armies spent the long, cold winter of 1863 trying to stay warm and fed. Some compared the filthy winter camp at Falmouth, Virginia, to Valley Forge, Pennsylvania, where George Washington's army had suffered through the harsh winter of 1777 and 1778 during the American Revolution.

As winter gave way to spring, President Lincoln chose yet another general to head the Union army. Both George McClellan and Ambrose Burnside had disappointed him, so Lincoln gave command to Joseph Hooker, known as "Fighting Joe." Immediately, Hooker cleaned up the camps, made sure his soldiers were fed, and designed and gave out badges to soldiers to boost morale.

General Joseph Hooker ▶ was given command of the Army of the Potomac after Ambrose Burnside's failures at the Battle of Fredericksburg. But Hooker failed to live up to his nickname, "Fighting Joe," in the Battle of Chancellorsville, where his retreat led to Robert E. Lee's last major victory.

Most important to Lincoln, Hooker promised to show no mercy for Lee's army.

Chancellorsville

At the end of April, Hooker led his troops toward Chancellorsville, a tangled woodland west of Fredericksburg, where Lee's army remained. Although Hooker had more men and was better supplied, Robert E. Lee and Stonewall Jackson had a better plan. Hooker was confused by the thick woods—known as the Wilderness—and decided to wait for more troops to arrive. This gave the Confederates enough time to divide their men, move them around, and confuse the Union troops.

The battle went on for three days, with eighteen thousand casualties on the Union side and nearly thirteen thousand on the Confederate side. Chancellorsville is remembered for one casualty in particular, however. On the moonlit night of May 2, Stonewall Jackson and a few other officers mounted their horses to scout the Union position. Nervous Confederate lookouts mistook Jackson for the enemy, shooting him in the right hand and left arm. He was moved to a field hospital, where his arm was amputated. In a weakened state, he soon caught pneumonia.

On May 10, Jackson died, and much of the Confederacy's confidence died with him. In his final moments, he began to give an order as if he were back on the battlefield, but stopped mid-sentence. His last words were, "Let us cross over the river and rest under the shade of the trees."[1]

Gettysburg

Joe Hooker's command was short-lived. By July, Lincoln replaced him with George Gordon Meade. Meade was a

Tools   Search   Notes   Discuss   Go!

hot-tempered Pennsylvanian, and it was fitting that his first major test would be on the fields near Gettysburg, Pennsylvania. Although the Battle of Antietam in Maryland had been disastrous, Lee had decided to take his army north once more.

With Jackson dead, Lee entrusted his three corps of soldiers to Confederate generals James Longstreet, A. P. Hill, and Richard Ewell. When they reached Gettysburg, the armies took up opposing positions on two parallel ridges that ran north to south through the town. The Union army claimed Cemetery Ridge, while the Confederate army set up on Seminary Ridge.

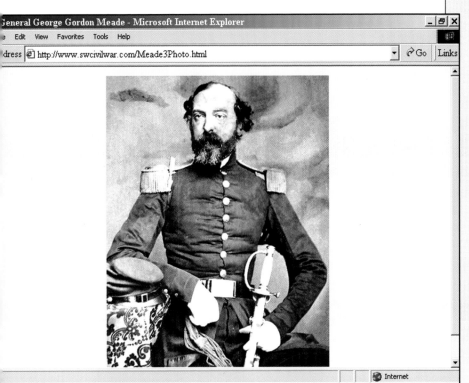

General George Gordon Meade - Microsoft Internet Explorer

Edit   View   Favorites   Tools   Help

Address http://www.swcivilwar.com/Meade3Photo.html   Go   Links

Internet

▲ *General George Gordon Meade, born in Spain of American parents, was assigned command of the Army of the Potomac only three days before the Battle of Gettysburg.*

The first day of the battle, July 1, happened almost by accident. General Ewell had heard that shoes were abundant in Gettysburg, and he moved toward the town to collect some for his men, who were sorely in need of them. There, Confederates ran headlong into Union troops, and they opened fire on each other. The

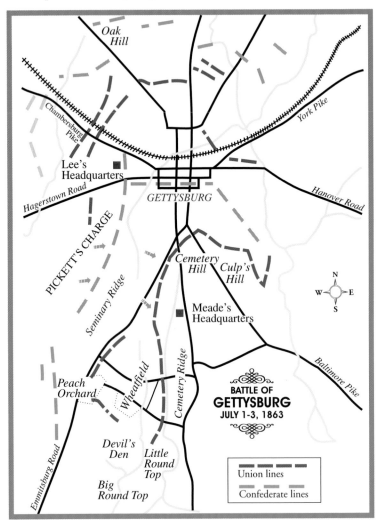

Oak Hill

Chambersburg Pike

York Pike

Lee's Headquarters

Hagerstown Road

GETTYSBURG

Hanover Road

PICKETT'S CHARGE

Seminary Ridge

Cemetery Hill   Culp's Hill

Meade's Headquarters

N
W — E
S

Peach Orchard

Wheatfield

Cemetery Ridge

Baltimore Pike

BATTLE OF
GETTYSBURG
JULY 1-3, 1863

Devil's Den   Little Round Top

Emmitsburg Road

Big Round Top

Union lines
Confederate lines

▲ The battleground of the war's pivotal battle, the Battle of Gettysburg, is shown in this map. The Confederate forces were to the north, and the Union forces were south of the town.

Confederates drove the Yankees backward to two hills on the north end of Cemetery Ridge.

When the Confederates renewed their attack the following morning, Union troops were in excellent positions on high ground. The day's most memorable struggle took place on Little Round Top, at the very opposite end of the Union line, where only a handful of Union regiments defended the hill against waves of charging rebels. One of these units, the 20th Maine, commanded by Joshua L. Chamberlain, led a brave counterattack that unexpectedly stopped the rebel advance.

On the battle's third day, Lee made the fateful decision to attack the center of the Union line. Under the leadership of George Pickett, for whom the charge was named, and two other commanders, fifteen thousand men crossed an open field a mile wide. But Meade's men were waiting for the coming soldiers with rifles and cannons. More than half the rebels who charged were killed, wounded, or captured. Some units were completely destroyed.

With Lee accepting all the blame for the loss, his army returned to Virginia. Lee would never again venture into northern territory. In three days, more than fifty-one thousand soldiers had been killed and wounded. Lee was so devastated that he offered to resign his post, but Jefferson Davis refused to accept his resignation.

That November, President Lincoln traveled to Gettysburg to dedicate what had become a national cemetery. It was at that dedication that he delivered his famous address at Gettysburg, honoring the soldiers who had died, giving "the last full measure of devotion" to the Union cause. "The world will little note, nor long remember what we say here," Lincoln said, "but it can never forget what they did here."[2]

Vicksburg

The day after the Union army claimed victory at Gettysburg, Union troops under Ulysses S. Grant forced the Confederate surrender of Vicksburg, a key port on the Mississippi River. For months, Grant had fired on the city, forcing its residents into cellars and even caves, until it finally crumbled on July 4. The Union controlled the Mississippi for the rest of the war, and some angry Vicksburg citizens would not celebrate Independence Day for the next eighty-two years.

Fort Wagner

Encouraged by the Union victories, increasing numbers of African-American soldiers (then referred to as "colored") joined the Union army in the summer of 1863. By the end of the war, 180,000 had joined in the fight.

On July 18, 1863, the 54th Massachusetts Infantry, which included two sons of Frederick Douglass, fought in one of the war's most memorable battles. Directed by their white commander, Colonel Robert Gould Shaw, the 54th led a charge against Fort Wagner, part of the defenses of Charleston, South Carolina. Under heavy fire, most of the 54th made it over the fort's walls, where they engaged in hand-to-hand combat with the Confederates. More than half of the regiment were killed, including Shaw. But because of its bravery, the 54th Massachusetts became the most famous African-American regiment of the Civil War.

Chickamauga and Chattanooga

In September, the Confederates staged a brutal assault on Union forces at Chickamauga, Georgia, that resulted in almost thirty-five thousand casualties. There, a stubborn

Union general named George H. Thomas, a native Virginian, managed a brave stand in the face of attacking Confederates. Ordering his soldiers to build earthworks as fast as they could, Thomas became known as "the Rock of Chickamauga."

As 1863 drew to a close, the Union army had begun to wear down the Confederates. Although the rebels had won at Chickamauga, they lost a key battle at nearby Chattanooga, Tennessee, only two months later. That October, Lincoln gave Ulysses Grant, who had led his soldiers to victories from Fort Henry to Chattanooga, command of the Military Division of the Mississippi,

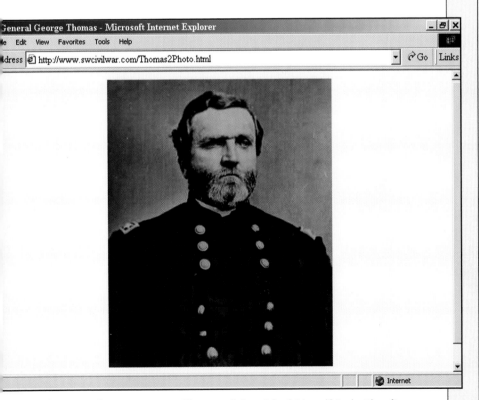

General George Thomas - Microsoft Internet Explorer

File Edit View Favorites Tools Help

Address http://www.swcivilwar.com/Thomas2Photo.html ▾ Go Links

Internet

▲ *General George Henry Thomas distinguished himself in battle after battle, especially at Chickamauga where his men held fast against what seemed insurmountable odds.*

which gave him control of all Union military operations from the Mississippi River east to the mountains. On March 10, 1864, General Grant was made General-in-Chief of the U.S. Armies.

Wilderness and Spotsylvania

Now in charge of all Union forces, Grant's plan was to wear down the Confederate army, soldier by soldier. In May 1864, a year after they had tangled at Chancellorsville, the armies battled each other again in the same woodlands, which they called the Wilderness. A week later, they clashed at nearby Spotsylvania Court House. Even after three years of warfare, veterans were shocked at the fierceness of the Spotsylvania battle. "I never expect to be fully believed when I tell what I saw of the horrors of Spotsylvania," a Union officer wrote later.[3] According to several accounts, the gunfire was so thick that it felled oak trees.

Although both battles were fought to a draw, Grant had succeeded in causing heavy casualties in the already-battered Confederate

Following the Union defeat at Cold Harbor, General Grant changed his battle plan, deciding not to try direct strikes at Richmond, Virginia.

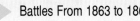
army, even though he lost more men. Grant's eyes were fixed on the Confederate capital at Richmond, and the rebels dug in their heels.

Cold Harbor

In June, Richmond saw one of the war's deadliest battles. Sensing Grant's resolve, Confederates had begun to dig trenches and build earthworks to protect themselves from attack. Miles of trench lines crisscrossed Richmond, including a vital crossroads known as Cold Harbor that was situated ten miles northeast of the Confederate capital. There, the entrenched rebels had only 59,000 men to face 109,000 attacking Union troops. Despite their greater numbers, the Union troops were doomed. Hundreds of Union soldiers pinned notes to their uniforms with their names and addresses so they could be identified if they were killed. Many were—in only half an hour, the Union army suffered more than six thousand casualties. In his memoirs, Ulysses S. Grant admitted, "I have always regretted that the last assault at Cold Harbor was ever made."[4] Before a cease-fire was negotiated, more than 13,000 Union soldiers and 3,000 Confederate soldiers had been killed or wounded. The Battle of Cold Harbor had been a Confederate victory, but it would be Lee's last major victory.

Sherman's March to the Sea

As the armies fought for Richmond in the north, Union general William Tecumseh Sherman had begun a slow advance toward Atlanta, Georgia, the heart of the Deep South. Along the way, his army was a constant thorn in the side of Confederate general Joseph Johnston, who was forced to retreat several times as Sherman got closer to Atlanta. Sherman's men entered Atlanta on the last day of August,

destroying mile after mile of railroad track, burning buildings, and forcing citizens to run for their lives.

Then, Sherman began his famous "march to the sea." His plan was to march through Georgia to the coastal city of Savannah, destroying as much Confederate property on the way as he could. As waged by Sherman, war was no longer just two armies shooting at each other across an open field—it meant months of siege warfare and the destruction of homes and businesses.

Although devastating for the South, Sherman's march was celebrated in a song by Henry Clay Work called "Marching through Georgia," which had a joyous chorus:

> Hurrah! Hurrah! We bring the jubilee!
> Hurrah! Hurrah! The flag that makes you free!
> So we sang the chorus from Atlanta to the sea,
> While we were marching through Georgia.[5]

As thousands of former slaves followed the Union troops, the Army began to sense that victory would soon be theirs.

◁ *When Ulysses S. Grant was made commander-in-chief of all Union armies, General William Tecumseh Sherman was made commander of the armies in the West. His Atlanta campaign and the path of destruction carved by his troops on their march to Savannah left the state of Georgia in ruins.*

Chapter 5

The Final Battles: Late 1864 to Spring 1865

After they reached the sea, Sherman's men marched north into the Carolinas. Meanwhile, the Union army had settled in at Petersburg, Virginia, for what would become a ten-month siege, beginning in June 1864 and lasting until the end of the war. Their aim was to cut off the rebel supply lines and force the South to surrender or starve.

Both Union and Confederate soldiers had built trenches and earthworks for their defense that formed a semicircle around the south side of Petersburg. For months, the armies clashed again and again, as Grant's forces slowly weakened the Confederate army.

▶ The Crater

A portion of the Confederate line was targeted in a Union mining operation that resulted in the Battle of the Crater on July 30, 1864. One of the most creative attacks of the Civil War, the Crater resulted from a Union plan to dig a tunnel below the Confederate line, pack it with gunpowder, and blow a hole in the rebel defenses. The tunnel, dug mostly by coal miners turned soldiers, took a month to dig and was 511 feet long. When the powder exploded, it created a giant crater 30 feet deep and up to 170 feet wide. More than 275 Confederates were instantly killed. But instead of taking the advantage, confused Union officers ordered their troops, including a division of African-American soldiers, to advance into the crater's tunnel. There, the Confederates easily targeted them, inflicting

▲ *These Union soldiers are seen waiting in trenches, during the siege of Petersburg.*

more than four thousand casualties. The plan was brilliant in theory but doomed in execution.

Lincoln's Reelection

In November 1864, Abraham Lincoln was reelected president by a wide margin—earning 212 of 233 electoral votes. Nearly 80 percent of all Union soldiers voted for Lincoln, even though many had great affection for his opponent, former U.S. Army commander George McClellan.

In his second inaugural address, Lincoln urged Americans "to bind up the nation's wounds; to care for him who shall have borne the battle and for his widow, and his orphan—to do all which may achieve and cherish a just and a lasting peace among ourselves, and with all nations."[1]

The Fall of the Confederacy

On April 1, 1865, a desperate battle took place at Five Forks, a road junction located to the southwest of

Petersburg, that was the last remaining supply route into the city. There, Lee's forces were outnumbered by a ratio of two to one and were easily defeated by Grant's men. The next day, the final assault on Petersburg began. After months of siege warfare, the Union army broke through the Confederate line, sending Lee's army running. Petersburg was soon in Union control, and Richmond fell soon after.

The tattered remains of the Confederate army retreated west toward Appomattox Court House.

The End at Appomattox

Appomattox Court House was a country village in south-central Virginia. These peaceful hillsides felt safe, especially to Wilmer McLean, who had moved there from his farm in Manassas to escape the war. With the First Battle of Manassas, the war had begun in his front yard. Now it was going to end in his front parlor.

The Yankees did not allow the Confederates to leave Richmond and Petersburg without a fight. As the armies moved west toward Appomattox, they clashed several times, with an especially costly battle at Sailor's Creek that resulted in 7,700 Confederate casualties.

Wanting no more loss of life, Grant sent Lee a respectful request that he surrender. At first, Lee refused. But after a brief battle in Appomattox killed and wounded more soldiers, Lee knew that all was lost. "There is nothing left for me to do but to go and see General Grant," he said, "and I would rather die a thousand deaths."[2]

Lee and Grant exchanged messages and agreed to meet in Wilmer McLean's home on April 9, which happened to be Palm Sunday. Lee dressed carefully, wearing his best sword and a red sash. Ever the field soldier, Grant wore his

Even in defeat, General Robert E. Lee was loved and admired by his men.

mud-spattered uniform. After some polite conversation, the two generals soon turned to the terms of surrender. Grant's terms were merciful. He allowed Confederate officers to keep their pistols, and soldiers who owned horses could take them home. "This will have the best possible effect upon the men," Lee said.[3] They exchanged good-byes and parted.

Although the two armies had years' worth of bitterness, they also had tremendous respect for each other. On April 12, Joshua L. Chamberlain—the hero of Little Round Top—accepted the formal surrender of the Confederate infantry. He ordered the Union boys to raise their arms in salute, an honor the rebels returned. "[They were] standing before us now, thin, worn, and famished, but erect and with eyes looking level into ours, waking memories that bound us together as no other bond," Chamberlain later wrote, "—was not such manhood to be welcomed back into a Union so tested and assured?"[4]

The Aftermath

Lee's surrender did not entirely end the Civil War. It would take several more weeks before all the remaining armies in the field gave up their arms. But that did not stop joyous citizens throughout the North from celebrating. In Washington, D.C., fireworks erupted in the sky, and a crowd gathered at the White House, demanding that Lincoln give a speech. Instead, the weary president asked that the band play "Dixie," the famous song of the South. He called it "one of the best tunes I ever heard."[1]

The celebration did not last long. On April 14, a deranged actor and Southern sympathizer named John Wilkes Booth shot Lincoln while he and his wife, Mary, attended a play called *Our American Cousin* at Ford's Theatre in Washington. Lincoln was carried across the street to a home, where his tall body was placed diagonally across a bed. Doctors quickly saw that the wound was fatal.

On the morning of April 15, surrounded by his wife and members of his cabinet, the nation's sixteenth president, who had preserved the Union after four perilous and deadly years, died.

An Emotional Response

As a long funeral journey brought Lincoln's body to its final resting place in Illinois, the American flag hung at half-staff at the White House. John Wilkes Booth was cornered in a barn and killed by Union troops, but this could not lift the

Abraham Lincoln, the man who had preserved the Union and steered the country through four years of civil war, would not live to see the nation reunited.

nation's sorrow. As the surviving soldiers came home, families both North and South grieved for their loved ones who had been lost on the battlefields. In four years, more than 620,000 soldiers had died, either in combat or from disease.

But the reunited nation was also glad that the bloodshed had ended. As the government worked to rebuild the nation in a period called Reconstruction, a Grand Review of the Union armies was planned for Washington, D.C. On May 23, 1865, flags were raised to full staff for the first time since Lincoln's death, and 150,000 Union soldiers marched down Pennsylvania Avenue from the Capitol toward the White House. Joshua Chamberlain was amazed at the parade of soldiers, these "men from far and wide, who with heroic constancy, through toils and sufferings and sacrifices that can never be told, had broken down the Rebellion. . . ."[2]

▶ Constitutional Changes

The Civil War resulted in several important amendments to the U.S. Constitution. The Thirteenth Amendment, which was ratified, or approved, in 1865, formally ended

Tools   Search   Notes   Discuss   Go!

slavery throughout the United States. The Fourteenth Amendment, ratified in 1868, guaranteed citizenship to all persons born or naturalized in the United States. And the Fifteenth Amendment, ratified in 1870, declared that a citizen's right to vote could not be denied based on race, color, or previous condition as a slave.

It took the civil rights movement of the 1950s and 1960s—a full century after the Civil War—to enforce racial equality not only in the South but in all of the country.

A New Nation

The Civil War changed the United States in many ways. The war produced advances in military tactics and in medicine. Hospitals improved sanitary conditions. Anesthesia, the use of medicine to remove pain during surgery, and the use of ambulances to aid and transport people needing medical care came from the war. It was also the first American war in which photographers shot battlefield scenes, which were printed in newspapers. The war ushered in a new industrial economy, with many cities in the Northeast benefiting from the production of goods to support the conflict.

Most importantly, however, the Civil War united the country in a way that it had not been united before. After the war, the term *Union* was hardly ever used, as if it were a painful reminder of that bloody conflict. In his Gettysburg Address, Abraham Lincoln signaled the change, using the word *nation* five times. That word was important to Lincoln, who sought above everything else to bring the country back together, making it the kind of strong nation that its forefathers had envisioned. The nation that was preserved was not done so without great cost, but that it was preserved was because in battle after battle, Americans gave their lives for what they believed.

Chapter 1. The Bloodiest Day

1. Geoffrey Ward with Ric Burns and Ken Burns, *The Civil War* (New York: Vintage Books, 1994), p. 129.

Chapter 2. The First Shots

1. James M. McPherson, *Battle Cry of Freedom: The Civil War Era* (New York and Oxford: Oxford University Press, 1988), p. 203.

2. Geoffrey Ward with Ric Burns and Ken Burns, *The Civil War* (New York: Vintage Books, 1994), p. 33.

Chapter 3. The Rise of the South: Battles From 1861 to 1862

1. James M. McPherson, *For Cause & Comrades: Why Men Fought in the Civil War* (New York and Oxford: Oxford University Press, 1997), p. 23.

2. James M. McPherson, *Battle Cry of Freedom: The Civil War Era* (New York and Oxford: Oxford University Press, 1988), p. 342.

3. McPherson, *For Cause & Comrades: Why Men Fought in the Civil War*, p. 87.

4. Frances H. Kennedy, ed., *The Civil War Battlefield Guide,* second ed. (Boston and New York: Houghton Mifflin, 1998), p. 111.

5. Robert E. Lee to James Longstreet, December 13, 1862, at the Battle of Fredericksburg, *The Columbia World of Quotations* (New York: Columbia University Press, Bartelby.com, 2000), <www.bartleby.com/66/69/35269.html> (August 14, 2003).

Chapter 4. The North Pushes Back: Battles From 1863 to 1864

1. Geoffrey Ward with Ric Burns and Ken Burns, *The Civil War* (New York: Vintage Books, 1994), p. 174.

2. Frances H. Kennedy, ed., *The Civil War Battlefield Guide*, second edition (Boston and New York: Houghton Mifflin, 1998), p. 215.

3. James M. McPherson, *Battle Cry of Freedom: The Civil War Era* (New York and Oxford: Oxford University Press, 1988), p. 731.

4. Ulysses S. Grant, *Personal Memoirs* (New York: C. L. Webster, 1885–1886; Bartleby.com, 2000), <www.bartleby.com/1011/> (August 14, 2003).

5. Richard Marius, ed., *The Columbia Book of Civil War Poetry: From Whitman to Walcott* (New York: Columbia University Press, 1994), p. 106.

Chapter 5. The Final Battles: Late 1864 to Spring 1865

1. Geoffrey Ward with Ric Burns and Ken Burns, *The Civil War* (New York: Vintage Books, 1994), pp. 294–295.

2. Frances H. Kennedy, ed., *The Civil War Battlefield Guide*, second edition (Boston and New York: Houghton Mifflin, 1998), p. 431.

3. Ibid.

4. Joshua Lawrence Chamberlain, *The Passing of the Armies* (New York: Bantam Books, 1993), p. 195.

Chapter 6. The Aftermath

1. Geoffrey Ward with Ric Burns and Ken Burns, *The Civil War* (New York: Vintage Books, 1994), pp. 309–310.

2. Joshua Lawrence Chamberlain, *The Passing of the Armies* (New York: Bantam Books, 1993), p. 248.

Further Reading

Arnold, James R., and Roberta Wiener. *River to Victory: The Civil War in the West, 1861–1863.* Minneapolis: Lerner Publishing Group, 2002.

Chamberlain, Joshua Lawrence. *The Passing of the Armies.* New York: Bantam Books, 1993.

Freeman, Douglas Southall. *Lee* (Abridged). New York: MacMillan Publishing, 1991.

Furgurson, Ernest B. *Chancellorsville 1863: The Souls of the Brave.* New York: Alfred A. Knopf, 1992.

Hennessy, John. *Return to Bull Run: The Campaign and Battle of Second Manassas.* New York: Simon & Schuster, 1993.

Hughes, Christopher. *Antietam.* Brookfield, Conn.: Millbrook Press, Inc., 1998.

———. *Gettysburg.* Brookfield, Conn.: Millbrook Press, Inc., 1998.

Hull, Mary E. *The Union and the Civil War in American History.* Berkeley Heights, N.J.: Enslow Publishers, Inc., 2000.

Kennedy, Frances H., ed. *The Civil War Battlefield Guide,* second edition. Boston and New York: Houghton Mifflin, 1998.

McPherson, James M. *Battle Cry of Freedom: The Civil War Era.* New York and Oxford: Oxford University Press, 1988.

Smolinski, Diane. *Key Battles of the Civil War.* Chicago: Heinemann Library, 2002.

Ward, Geoffrey, with Ric Burns and Ken Burns. *The Civil War.* New York: Vintage Books, 1994.